Father Armando's work is a good example of a new movement in poetry, in Chicano poetry, that tends to the spiritual . . . Chicano poetry has dealt with a type of movement which was more political and more social. Father Armando's poetry contains that social context, not so much (explicitly) political, but (implicitly) political. The social and political elements are contained within his treatment of the spiritual; they are closely allied in his poetry. But the movement is more spiritual, more personal, and it shows that within the realm of the spiritual and poetry there is much to explore that hasn't been explored in Chicano poetry up to now.

-- Miguel R. Lopez, Ph.D.
Southern Methodist University

Ibáñez is definitely a dancer! He's a dancer-poet. I hope to choreograph dance to his poem entitled, Ruah.

-- Sr. Lisa Lopez Williams, O.P., liturgical dancer,
Berkeley

I have always seen the connection between poetry and the spiritual. Armando's poetry makes that connection very explicit . . . His poetry is so accessible, so readily understandable, his images so crisp and clear that the reader or listener is easily drawn in to the emotion or the story. . . In Armando's poetry we are brought a little closer to the realm of the spirit . . .

-- Nancy Greenfield, campus minister,
Stanford University

Wrestling

with the

Angel

-- A Collection of Poetry

by

Armando P. Ibáñez

Pluma Productions
Los Angeles, 1997

467

FIRST EDITION

Illustrations of angels on cover and section openings, called
Angel Playing, La Scala and are paintings by Fra Angelico
Giovanni (1387-1455).

Library of Congress Catalog Number: 96-92790

ISBN 1-889848-08-5

Published by
PLUMA PRODUCTIONS
A SUBSIDIARY OF THE
SOUTHERN DOMINICAN PROVINCE, USA

PLUMA PRODUCTIONS
1977 Carmen Ave.
Los Angeles, CA 90068

REVELATION

The revelation of God
Is Unfolding fire
Crackling, smoldering
In blinding smoke.

PREFACE

I don't like to explain my poetry. Poetry should speak for itself. However, I must note my usage of English-Spanish -- more commonly known as *Tex-Mex*. (English translations are provided in parenthesis.) Some call this interchangeable style *Tex-Mex or Spanglish*. Many linguists call it "code-switching."

The important thing is that many people in the Southwest, especially Chicanos in South Texas, speak in all English, all Spanish and in *Tex-Mex*. It is a reality. Thus, many years ago, I decided to reflect this reality by composing some of my poetry in *Tex-Mex*. I decided to do so because I believe one of a poet's primary responsibilities is to reflect reality as best as he or she knows how.

ACKNOWLEDGMENTS

I am most thankful to my Dominican brothers and sisters for their much-needed support, especially my brothers of the Southern Dominican Province. Without their prayers and support this book would not have been possible.

I am also grateful to Michelle Macau, a close friend, for her support, love and friendship, and to Jorge Chavera, a good friend of mine, for his many hours of listening to many of my poems through the years. I also thank Leo Carrillo for his encouragement and idea of illustrating this book with angels. My thanks also to Chrys Finn, O.P., for his great help in securing the angel illustrations, José Alberto Bagué for proof-reading, and Michael O'Rourke, O.P., for his computer expertise.

Finally, my warm thanks to my good friend and fellow poet Chris Renz, O.P., and the rest of the poets in the Power of Poetry -- A Celebration.

I'd like to recognize the following publications for having published the works listed below. They are:

A Passing Light, A Gathering Storm, and *Mi Angel* were published in my first book of poetry, Midday Shadows, in 1980. *To Melt* was published by Writer's Block, *Texas A&I University,* Kingsville, Texas, in 1983. *Olas del Mar* and *Mesquites Never Die,* were published by Aciendo Harte, a publication of the *Center for Hispanic Arts,* Corpus Christi, Texas, in its 1986 Winter anthology. *A Stirring Wind* and *Peering,* were published in the 1987 Winter edition of Aciendo Harte.

Mesquites Never Die, A Stirring Wind and Peering were also published by *Preacher's Exchange* in its issues of January, 1989, May, 1989, and November, 1989, respectively. *Preacher's Exchange* also published: *Sunlight Harp,* February, 1989; *Flame,* January, 1990; *In Search of Nakedness,* May, 1990; *Light* and *A Summons,* January, 1991; *Al Amar,* May, 1991; *I Hear You, Lord,* September, 1991; *Una Copa,* January, 1992; *Revelation,* February, 1992; *Waiting,* November 1993; and *Misterio,* December, 1993. *Ruah* was published by *Ruah,* 1993 issue, and *A Summons* in the 1995 issue.

Question, The Little Sparrow and *Grace* were published by *The Poet's Pen,* 1995 Summer issue.

A Él -- el lindisimo Dios -- y en memoria de mis queridos padres, Gerónimo y Vicenta, y de mis hermanos, Guillermo y Ricardo.

Contents

Part III

Part IV

Wrestling

with the

Angel

I
The Search

QUESTION

I ask you, Eternal One,
Am I to be another corpse
In a pile of what-was
And is no more?

There are moments
I must confess
When I truly do not know.
And yet there are others
When I touch and feel the warmth
of an elusive beam of light.

Freedom — Freedom?

One afternoon I sat by a pond
And saw my reflection
study my face,
My eyes.

"Are you free?,"
my reflection asked me
through ringlets of breathing water.

My shadow sat beside me.

"Free? Of course, I'm free!,"
I half-chuckled at the question,
but was amazed that my reflection
could speak.

"How can you answer a question so quickly,
a question which may have no answer?,"
my reflection inquired,
and looked intently at my shadow.

What could I say?
I was frozen in stillness.
My shadow waded its feet
Into the water.

"Now, come with me on a journey,"
My reflection invited me,
"On a journey of questions,
Propelled by one question:
"What is freedom?' "

My shadow dived into the water.

Sea

Sea,
Oh Sea,
Gulf within me,
Your waters
Have the power
To arouse
And calm me.

I sit on the shores
Esperando   (Waiting)
Viendo   (Watching)
Sintiendo   (Feeling)
el viento   (The breeze)
Go through my nostrils
And
Inflame my soul.

Agua pura,   (Pure Water)
Cristalina,   (Crystal clear)
Tu que llevas   (You who take
 Y trais   (And give)
The Breath of Life,
Don't forget me.

Sea,
Oh sea,
Gulf within me,
Your waters
Have the power
To arouse
And calm me.

Así como tú   (Just like you)

5

He tratado de dar	(I have tried to give)
Vida	(Life)
Y a veces I have succeeded	(And at times)
Pero en otras —	(But on other times)
El fracaso,	(The failure)
The miserable failures.	

Priests and poets	
A veces	(At times)
Han sido los peores.	(Have been the worst)
A dar amor y	(To be loving and)
compasión	(Compassionate)
A veces son	(At times are)
Nada más	(Nothing more)
Than words,	
Hollow,	
Fragile	
Shattering into flying pieces	
As the cheap flask	
Hits the floor.	

Sea,
Oh Sea,
Gulf within me
Your waters
Have the power
To arouse
And calm me.

Mar,	(Sea)
Dadora de vida,	(Giver of life)
You who have witnessed	
The Clothed Beast,	
The Thinking man,	
Bash	

The brains of fellow man,
Look upon
The tear of the Naked Man —
La Flor,   (The Flower)
The delicate flower
Striving within.

Look
At the marching armies
Hovering helicopters
And loaded machine guns
Spread
Their "good tidings of
Freedom, peace, humanity and love,"
As a balloon-belly child
Withers into a thin, flaccid
Bag of flesh and bone.

Sea,
Oh sea,
Gulf within me,
Your waters
Have the power
To arouse
And calm me.

Espero   (I await)
El viento,   (The wind)
El tiempo   (The time)
A ver   (To see)
Si por fin   (Whether finally)
I have learned,
We have learned,
The mute, serene message
De la Flor.   (The Flower)

7

The Little Sparrow

Where are you going, little sparrow?
At times, I don't want to know.

You, yourself, don't know
Because at times you go where
The wind blows.

Where are you going?
Who supports your wings?
You don't know.
You only know that you're on
Your way.

Where are you going, little sparrow?
Remember that the wind
Can change
And throw you back
From where you came or
To a place of dreams.

Where are you going, little sparrow?

Ruah

Ruah stretched her wings
Underneath her cloak of darkness.

Se sonrío	(She smiled)
Y su sonrisas reventó	(And her smile)
En explosiones	(Burst in explosions)
De luz.	(Of light)

The stars, countless suns
Spun in a frenzy of dance —
Explosions of light and fire.

Lumbre, heat,	(Fire)
frío, warmth	(Cold)

fire.
She gazed at the sight,
giggled in delight,
and threw off her cloak of darkness,
which became the heavens.
She danced!
The horizons — planets
appeared at every footstep.
Ruah,

Que dulce son tus pies.	(Your feet are so sweet.)

She spun.
She danced.

Bailando,	(Dancing,)
Cantando	(Singing)
Y con risas	(And with warm)
calientitas	(laughter)

Ruah spun,
spun in sheer ecstasy
Until from her womb
the earth came forth.

9

Pausó.   (She paused.)

Se sentó   (She sat down)
a ver su criatura.   (to examine her creation.)
She kissed the earth.
And water was born — life.

Con sus manos   (With her hands)
empezó   (She began)
a jugar   (To play)
con el lodo y agua   (with the soil and water)
-- zoquete.   (— mud)
Plants,
animals and all sorts
of living things
oozed out from
between her fingers.
She laughed.

She paused.
She held a clump of mud, lifeless clay.
"Man," she said,
Breathing into the clay.
"Go, and become humanity."

First Breath

Are we mere bodies
gathering soil beneath our feet?
I ask and wonder
to what end is the purpose
of roaming bone and flesh?

A soul,
a spirit,
is said to thrive
in our palpitating flesh.

It breathes
and lives
since the first breath
was released
into hollow lips.

Oh,
ball of fire
your time will come
when this mass of flesh
becomes obsolete.
But before that time
you will crawl
walk
and stumble upon
countless mirrors
casting reflections of yourself
and illusions
of the soil beneath your feet.

Plunging in Flight

Leaves sighed,
Branches heaved —
Wind.
Silencio.   (Silence.)

In the deep crevices of my soul
I plunged
In flight,
Soaring,
Gliding,
Volando entre   (Flying amid)
 Miedo y confianza —   (Confidence and fear —)
La fe.   (The Faith.)

Fear and faith,
I hold my tears in glass jars.
I drink some of them in the shadows
Of my laughter
And others I shatter against the trees!

My Lord,
My God,
To love, you say,
Is to fly through the gray
Choking cloud of ridiculing fear
And to embrace you.
To love is what you ask of us.
Love?
Oh Force, where are you?
Fleeing in some emergency room?,
Holding a shaking bedpan?

Are you in an old woman's eyes

Seeking to pray?
But no one is there
To join her in her mumbles and
Groans.

Or are you in the man's breath?
When he said,
"I don't care, chaplain,
Whether you come or go."

And he tossed his rash-ridden
Legless torso
On its side.

Love,
What are you?
Where do you breathe?
What is my bread?
What is my drink?

My Lord,
My God,
Why the tears?
The fears,
The horrors, the sufferings,
The agony of dying?
Why does life end in tears?

Where are you Lord?
My God,
I am compelled to find you.
Where are you?
In me?
In her?
In him?

Where?

Deep,
Deep
I fly amidst
The clouds of my fears,
My doubts,
My hate.
Oh,
Don't hold the mirror
So close to me,
My God.

Where are you God?
I smell your breath
But I can't see you here.
Oh Lord,
Must I fly through
The clouds of my fears — tears?

Leaves sighed.

Height, Depth

What pain
What delight
When God's whirlwind swirls
Around us
And lifts us up to heights
We fear.
Yet, how else would
We learn to fly?

What horror
What ecstasy
When the air we breathe
Plunges us into
The darkness of uncertainty.
Yet, it is in our groping,
In our kneeling,
That our heart recognizes
The light lingering in the shadows.

Olas del Mar

Las olas del mar con	(The waves of the sea)
Serenatas de plata	(Serenaded with songs)
Cantaban	(Of silver)
A las sea gulls	(To the)
Who floated	
in an aqua sky.	

Las olas	(The waves)
with their flying white hair	
Crashed	
on an abandoned beach	
As *el sol*	(The sun)
Lloraba con lagrimas	(wept with tears)
de lumbre —	(of fire)
Aluzando	(Illuminating)
Aluzando,	
Aluzando.	

Y en la arena	(And in the sand)
Se revolcaba	(rolled)
A sandcrab	
Buscando,	(Searching)
Buscando,	
Buscando	

Until finally
    The tiny creature
        came across
        a pearl embedded in the corpse
           of a dead oyster.
    As the sea hurled itself against
    Porous sand
        the tiny creature
        held the pearl in his claw

Y las lágrimas　　　　　　　　(And the tears)
　　del sol　　　　　　　　　(of the sun)
　　relumbraban　　　　　　(shimmered)
　　on the face of the jewel.

The crab
　　took the pearl
And washed it
En las olas que brincaban　　(On the jumping waves)
Y con serenata　　　　　　(Serenaded:)
　　Cantaban:
　　　　"It was not in vain!"

17

II
The First Encounter

Encounters

It is in your eyes
Where I encounter
My reflections —
Myself
And
You are in mine.

A Lake

A lake stretched out
in yawns of sloshing sights
awakening from her evening sleep
and in humid whispers
beckoned me
to get a better look at the rising sun.
Accepting her invitation,
I boarded the leaning pier,
whose scraggly, gray legs
wobbled and creaked
in my chance-taking steps.

I looked up at the horizon and saw
a blinding sun,
painful to the eyes,
wrap himself in his cloak of white light
in the aqua, paling sky.
Streaks of oranges, pinks, violets and golds
splashed across the heavens —
a trumpeting call of colors
announcing the arrival of the sun.

"What do you see?,"
asked the lake in her wet breath.

I could taste
her echoing words riding in the breeze.
"The sun, the sun," I replied,
not knowing what else to say.

Suddenly,
darkness threw himself before me —
pain,
blotches,
my vision, my sight.
I looked away from the eye-piercing,
mesmerizing sun.

"Yes, the sun," the lake sloshed in reply.
"You have seen the sun."

Misterio

Poetry,
Misterio,
Mystery
Tú eres la oscuridad   (You are darkness)
de la luz.   (Of light)
Wherever you walk
I see my blindness
And am blinded by the light.
Mystery,
Misterio,
Shadow of light,
I feel your embraces in the night.
Whispering breath
seeping into my nostrils
I smell your words.
I utter.
I groan.

God, my Lord,
I see you dressed
in shadows and silhouettes.
Misterio,
You are here;
I am alone, naked — mystery.

24

Estas enamorado de mi.   (You are in love with me.)

How can I hug and kiss the wind?

Estoy solo.   (I am alone.)
You are here,
Misterio, naked.
Your beauty melts the
darkness into light
And the light into darkness —
Sight and blindness.
Oh, *misterio*, mystery,
You are *Misterio*.
Estoy enamorado de ti.   (I'm in love with you.)

A Summons

This night,
Fire has fallen
Upon the earth and is
Sizzling dry grass
Into its transparent curtain of heat,
While Breath emerges
From the crevices of the earth
And gazes upon Fire's eyes.

"I am fire, *Lumbre*," said Fire,
To eyes peering through
The darkness.

"I am Breath."

"I burn in you,"
Fire continued explaining
To the searching eyes.

"And I dance and whirl
In and out of you," added Breath,
While she stomped her bare feet
En la tierra, en el lodo.   (On the earth, on the mud.)

"Together we bring you life," they said,
And embraced
En una danza de amantes   (In a dance of naked lovers)
Desnudos.

"We are here to summon
The flames and breath
In you to join us in our embraces
Of a crackling, breathing fire,
To reach to the heavens,
To plunge into the
Depths of your souls
And let fire
Engulf your every thread."

They danced!
Bailaron.   (They danced.)
They dance.

And the earth
Bore her flowers —
Flowers of reds,
yellows,
blues and oranges
And violets and pinks.
They kissed the heavens.

Fire,
Breath,
Fire.

27

A Passing Light

A passing light
penetrated his being
blinding his eyes.
he fluttered them
trying to focus
but only blotches
of multicolored ink
appeared on the screen.

Oh!
What a light!
exploding in his inners
rushing to his heart
    his mind
        his soul!

What man is this
running through the brush
as vicious cactus plants
lower their shields
and fire their spears?

He runs
    flies
    jumps high
        high, high,
            high to the sky
while the cool breath
of the moon
soothes his wild heart.

Slowly,
Slowly,

gently he floats down
down to the bosom of the earth
to nurse again
only feeling
a warm sensation
of ashes past.

Sunlight Harp

The sun's illuminating
Strands
Came down from the pale blue heavens.

The green,
Crisp,
Vibrant grass
Took hold of the sun's golden web
And a grasshopper sitting
On a sprouting mushroom
Began to play on
The heaven's radiant harp.

His sweet song
Enchanted a floating leaf
To sway
To the beat of the soothing song.

Moon Breath

I breathed in the moon's
Silver light
Y me reí.   (And I smiled.)

Me dijo unas cosas   (She told me things)
Sin palabras.   (Without words.)
Eran unos secretos   (They were secrets)
Que corrían   (That ran)
Entre las sombras   (Through the shadows)
And hid
Behind the cool evening breeze.

A Well

A well
Carved deep into the brittle crust
Of stone-earth
Calls with humid, echoing words
Hard to understand.

Must I drop this bucket
Into your mouth
To draw water?
Is there an easier way?
After all, there are faucets,
There is bottled mineral water.
Why should I listen to your
Ringing call?

Suddenly,
The wind swirled her skirts
Around me
And I sensed a presence
Sit across from me.

"Give me something to drink,"
A voice told me.

Waiting

Waiting,
Esperando,   *(Waiting)*
Waiting
For those eyes
I drank in gulps and sips
Those eyes I ran away from
In fear,
In disbelief.

Lagrimas,   (Tears,)
Agua salada,   (Salty water,)
Escurres   (You ooze)
Tus huellas calientitas   (Your warm trails)
En las esquinas   (Over the corners)
de mi boca.   (Of my mouth.)

Esperando,   (Waiting)
Waiting,
Esperando
Que tu resuello   (For your breath
Se mezcle   (To mingle)
Con el mio   (With mine)
A darnos palabritas   (Sharing sweet nothings,)
Palabras,   (Words,)
Words.

I ate your words,
Slices of your breath,
In my dreams of you.
I laughed,
I sang,
I fell in love with you.
Now, I await.

Esperando,   (Waiting)
Awaiting
For your eyes,
Your face, to ignite
My laughter into songs once more,
My lover.

A Stirring Wind

A rushing wind
Caresses my temples
As its lips of rain-soaked soil
        Kiss my forehead and
        Awaken my nostrils
            To its invigorating breath.

I breathe
And move to the beat of
            Whispering buffalo grass and
            Dancing mesquites.

Oh, stirring wind,
Don't ever leave me
            In echoing stillness
But continue to
            Rush through my pores.
If for a moment you are
A faint beat of a lonely leaf,
            It will be sufficient.
If for a moment you are
But a flutter of a passing butterfly,
            That will be enough
For even then
            You are a stirring wind.

III
The Struggle -- Life, Death

To Melt

Even a cube of ice
can melt
and become water
giving life
to those
who thirst for it.

Ah,
but to melt
that's the question.

Light

The shadows,
The shadows,
The shadows.

Ah, yes!
Then there must be
Light.

Flame

Flames
Reaching skyward,
    Crackling
With their feet
Of oranges, yellows and blues
To consume
    To destroy,
        To give birth
           To give life.

The pain,
    The sorrow,
        The tears,
Oh, fire,
Your hot embraces
        are at times unbearable.
Yet,
I must breathe your searing heat
        for there is life!

The consuming fire will soon be gone.
    No more wood to burn,
    No more bark.
Ashes.
Powder of what-was
    is flying skyward in swirls of howling gusts
And, at times, floating in the silent caresses
        of a sweet-scented breeze.

Oh, steady Flame,
Non-consuming fire,
You're the blinding flame
           I seek.

I Hear You, Lord

I hear you breathing, Lord,
Inhaling and exhaling.
Yet, how can I speak of you?
Preach of your breath
With my words which even fail to describe
Stirrings within?
I can't even speak of the life of clicking rain,
Whispering snow.

But I feel you within!

Fly, you say?
Fly?
To fly, yes, to fly!
A volar contigo   (To fly with you)
Es lo que sigo   (Is what I seek)
A volar, volar,   (To fly, fly,)
Volar alto contigo   (Fly high with you)
Entre las nubes   (Through the clouds)
En lo clientito   (In the warmth)
del sol.   (of the sun.)

Let go,
Clinging hands —

Pale knuckles clutching purple.

Off we go!
Volando,   (Flying,)
Volando alto   (Flying high)
Tan alto,   (So high,)
Tan bajo.   (So low.)

I wrap my legs in the clouds,
Kiss the wind
Open my mouth and
Eat scoops of sweet fire.
Lumbre bendita,   (Holy Fire,)
Vamos volando alto   (We're flying high)
Tan alto   (So high)
Tan bajo.   (So low.)

Preaching,

Flying,
Predicando   (Preaching,)
Volando   (Flying)
Tan alto   (So high)
Tan alto   (So high)
Tan bajo.   (So low.)

Fire to Ashes

I am waiting
For the hands of eternal time
To comfort me
And make me understand
What has come to be —
Death, your death, my brother.
But at the moment I cannot see why
All is as it is:
The hurt, the tears,
The dry tears,
Silence.

The burning fire gathers intensity,
Defying the wind,
Who attempts to quiet
The fears of the roaring flame
With rushing embraces.
Oh wind,
The pain, of your embraces
Is searing my heart.
Don't you know that
The stronger your embrace
The hotter the fire?

Where can I run?
Where can I hide?
This didn't happen!
My brother didn't die,
Not now.
Why?

But you are gone, my brother.

Oh fire, oh fire,
My brother did die.
Fire, what do you want?
Is it the wind you fear?
Or are your flames licking skyward
In embers of terrified desire,
Seeking to understand death, birth?

Birth.

Yes, fire, burn, burn
Until you're nothing more than ashes —
Ashes rushing in whispering
Love songs to the wind.

A Gathering Storm

The clouds of a gathering storm
Cast their shadows
On scurrying figurines.

El aire frío   (The cold wind)
Whistled
Through the scrawny branches
Of petrified mesquite.

"¿Donde estas?,"   (Where are you?)
Howled the wind.

"Beast of beasts,
King of plastics,
And neon signs
Where do you
Cast
Your shadow?

In Search of Nakedness

There are times I wish
I were a child once more
to experience that
part of my life again,
not only to correct past mistakes,
but to giggle, laugh and play
through the unfolding veil of youth.
Ah,
to be naked again
without guilt or shame.

When I was a kid
I climbed trees,
not the tall ones
but the short ones,
played tag
and tied towels around my neck —
Superman!
Then, I also prayed.

Lord, my God,
where has time gone?
What have I done?

If I could,
I would harness time
to take me back
to my childhood
to board a cloud again
and to build dreams
out of mud and clay.
If I could, if I could . . .
Where are the trees?

Where are the mud and clay?
Where are you youth? —
a time gone in silent breaths.

My teens were
those wonderful years
of knowing-it-all,
a superman in a towel-less quest!
And, of course, my twenties
of roaring laughter,
a time of immortality!

Spent.

Youth,
I'd love to capture you again,
and I'd spend my hours
like a miser spends his pennies.

Oh, but then
I also remember
the pain,
the struggles,
the sorrows — the deaths.
I recall
the deaths of those I love
the painful deaths that
bore through my eyes
in convulsions of silent tears.
And, yes,
I too have died
many times — peeled raw.
No, youth,
I change my mind.
I'd much rather

have you tucked away
wrapped-up in romanticizing ribbons
of what-was and could've been
hidden in the calluses of my feet.

Now,
I look ahead
to continue unwrapping
time, and, hopefully,
unwrapping myself
until I am naked again.

To Embrace A Panhandler

One early morning
I sat outside a cafe
Sipping coffee.
Ah, I saw the sun's feathers
With all their splendor
Of red, violet, orange and golden
Wisps
Streak across the sky.
My God,
My Lord,
My God,
What beauty!

Then you,
An old, scraggly panhandler,
Sat at a table beside me.
Your stench
Insulted my quivering nostrils.
Your faded, gray overcoat
Stained in brown blotches of
Dried-up ketchup and filth
Brushed past me.
The stench,
The urine-tobacco-penetrated stench,

Rolled up against my throat.
I couldn't help but swallow a
Gulp of that salty-tasting stench!

Run away, I thought.
Give him a quarter so he'll go away.
Leave!
Yet, I stayed
Frozen in the cool, morning breeze.

I expected you to
Beg for my spare change
But you didn't.

Instead, you sipped your coffee
And puffed on a crooked cigarette
Oblivious to the morning sun
Except, perhaps, that another morning
Had ended a cold night on the streets.
Then, unaware of my presence
Or maybe you didn't care
You slurped your coffee,
Rubbed your grease-matted beard and left
Without a word,
Without a stare.

Although you repulsed me,
Panhandler,
The day will come
Must come
When we will embrace.

Where Were You God?

She held her eyeballs
Amid the stench,
the vomit
of having been gang-raped.
She could see the smile
of her child she held in her arms.

Al otro lado	(On the other side
de los reflejos	(of reflections)
Estaba un hombre	(A man)
Sentado	(Sat)

Holding his smile on his lap.
The pain, the pain, of ravaging AIDS
Bit at the corner of his mouth
And pounced on his eyelids.

Las sombras cubrían	(The shadows covered)
Al hombre y a la mujer	(The man and woman)
Aunque ellos	(Although they)
no se conocían.	(didn't know each other.)
Y los dos lloraban	(Both wept)
Con lágrimas secas	(With dry tears)
y gritos mudos.	(and mute sobs.)

God of Heaven
Where is your breath?
Your eyes?
Your arms?
Your scent?

On the night
she was ravaged,
A pack of wild men
Became enfleshed demons
Striking at her breasts,
Licking her with their
alcohol-pickled tongues
And dared to call it sex!
Their farts and wet armpits polluted
The air
As they humped their way to hell!

¿Donde estabas	(Where were
Dios Celestial?	(Heavenly God?)
¿Donde alzaste tus ojos?	(Where were your eyes?)
¿Con quien andabas?	(Who were you with?)
¿Qué no ves	(Can't you see)
con las estrellas?	(with the stars?)

The night before he died,
He cried out in excruciating pain:
"Take me, Lord, take me!"
The pain of illness,
The pain of accusing eyes,
The pain of decomposing human flesh
Struggling to exist.

Why?	
¿Por qué, Señor Jesús?	(Jesus, why?)

¿Donde estaba tu gracia?　　(Where was your grace?)
Where was your presence?
¿Donde estaba tu resuello?　(Where was your breath?)
In her?
In him?

In the silence of the corridors of my heart
I heard you weep, Jesus.
And you said:
"Can't you see it was I?
I am she
and I am he."

Hilos

My thoughts were peeled out
In webs of *hilo*   (thread)
Connecting with the heaving earth,
And the wet heavens.
Some eased upwards in the slight breath
of the wind.

Suddenly, I saw one running into
My father's loins,
Another into my mother's womb.
I was tied in webs of smoke,
But free,
Free to breathe my mother's breath
And walk away where ever
I felt Destiny's pulling gaze.

Threads, transparent threads,
Hilos of memory and union,
Your web is life — bread.

Ah, yes, there is death.
Death, how I hate you,
Loathe your gripping jaws.
How many have you killed?
All of them who were spun in thread
Have seen your eyes
And all of us
Still weaving
Will one day smell your stench
Of decaying flesh.
Disease, starvation, war,
Murder, old age
Are all licenses for you

To hunt us down.
We are your prey.

But don't be quick to cackle, Death,
Our *hilos* are far beyond your hands
Of squirming maggots and flies.
And one day we will wrap
Our umbilical cords around
Your screeching neck
Until you are dead!

Mesquites Never Die

I sat on a hill
Overlooking a grove of dancing mesquites
As a pale moon
Waved her platinum veil
To the beat of a distant drum.

A pink evening primrose struggled
To set her arms free
To join the dancers
Who paid no heed to the faint warning
Riding in the wind.

With their slender arms
The misunderstood ballerinas of ashen-bark
Reached up towards the watchful moon
Knowing that she understood
Their hearts, minds and souls.
Though they had the choice
To fade into the darkness
And exist among the shadows,
They danced —
Moving,
Swaying,
Tossing their green prickly hair
Amid the silver-blue pool
Relinquished by the moon's lingering veil.

The drums,
The beating drums,
Those drums
Kept rolling
Rolling,
Louder,

Louder,
Announcing their army
Just over the hill
To conquer
To destroy
For *righteousness*
and *love*!

As the pink evening primrose
Heard a trumpet blare its War-Cry
She pleaded with the mesquites.
She cried:
"Stop!
Stop your dancing
Or you will surely die!"

She screeched
And the drums
Died in silence.

The steel-pointed spears
Aligned themselves in neat rows
Across the horizon,
While the moon brightened
In her silver-fire
Warning the persistent mesquites
Who danced to the tune of a silent wind.

They whirled,
Swirled,
Turned,
Bowed to Mother Moon
And kissed the Earth.

"They're coming,

They're coming!
Please,
Please,
Stop
For surely the Clothed Beast
Will spare your lives,"
Pleaded the pink evening primrose.

A young mesquite turned to the pink flower
Who grew alongside his sculptured body
Kissed the blossom's warm tears
And said:
"We are who we are
Mesquites Dancing in the Wind."
"But the sword,"
Protested the flower.

"May make us bleed," he said,
Fanned the air with his long, slender fingers
And joined his brothers and sisters
In their soundless concert.

The drums suddenly rolled
Shattering the peacefulness of the night
Into crashing bits of glass.

The Army of Clothed Beasts
Descended
And with their golden swords,
Silver axes
And spears of steel
Hacked,
Chopped
Their way through the troupe of never-
surrendering dancers

Until not one stood in the platinum light.
A Sea of mangled bodies
And limbs
Lay behind the moving Army
As testimony of *Justice*,
Righteousness,
Love.

The pink evening primrose wept
Bitterly.

Through her salty tears
She saw the moon pick up scattered seeds
With her blue veil
And toss them
Into the gusty wind.

"Mesquites may bleed
But they never die!"

Peering

The pale face of the sun
        peered
        through a transparent mist
                lazily
                clinging
                to wet cotton fields.

On the horizon,
        pastel oranges
        and a faint violet-blue
clung
        to the glass dome above
        as a splash of lavender
snuggled up against
                still
                towering clouds.

"Oh, sun," whispered the wind,
        amid the scent of moist soil
        and dripping leaves,
        "when will your golden rays
                eliminate
                the persistent shadows?"

A Woman

There she sat
Eyes bathing in light.
"Hola, hermano."   (Hello, brother.)

Her legs
Her feet
Aligned side by side
Ready to move her thick body.
"¿Quieres rezar,   (Sister, would you
hermana?"   (like to pray?)

"Yes, I thank God," she said,
As a tear traced the deep line
Between her high cheeks and fat nose.
"For all the love, the blessings,
The Lord has given me."

¿Silencio — Silence —
Qué canción cantas   (What song do you sing)
en la oscuridad   (in the darkness)
De mis pensamientos?   (of my thoughts?)
What breath is this?
What stirs in this moment?

In her eyes?

Those legs
Those neat,
well-proportioned legs screamed —
Slapped my nostrils
Plastic!, plastic!
She has no legs!
Her breasts are almost gone,
Eaten away.
Her heart is about to stop.

"I can't explain," she smiled.
"The love, the strength, I feel in me.
Yes, I thank God for all the blessings
I have received."

Silence,
Silence,
Yes, I heard you sing.
God is here!

Oh Lord,
Help me strap on
My own plastic legs.

Drenching

The Heavens wept
Drenching
The earth with
God's tears.

IV
The Blessing

Una Copa

Yes, I hold up
Una copa.   (A cup)
I spilled my breath upon it
Y tu resuello   (And your breath
Se mezcló con el mío.   (Mingled with mine.)
We smiled.
We giggled.
We cried.

We lifted up the cup.
You drank.
I drank.
We cried.
We laughed in tears —
Lágrimas de sal.   (Tears of salt.)

The Discovery of a Bridge

The bridge, a bridge,
has been found!

My faith,
My love,
Mi Amor,   (My Love,)
I have found a place
To cross
And throw my arms around you.

Mi experiencia,   (My experience,)
Mi fe,   (My faith,)
My love,
Es el puente,   (Is the bridge)
Mi Amor.   (My Love)

En Buscas

Empecé
En buscas de palabras
Para desahogarme
De los sentimientos de mis
Padres.

Un libro.
No, libros y libros
De versos —
Poesía de la Rosa de Sangre y agua pura
iba a escribir.

Puse mis ojos al cielo
Y miré al sol cubriéndose
En rostros de nubes pasajeras.

Entre las lágrimas de luz
Que caían a medio día
Vi
A la Rosa de Sangre
Tomando su copa de agua pura.
Al verme aquella flor
Me dijo:
«Tu padre y madre
viven en la tierra,
Corren con el agua,
Suben Con las nubes,
Y aluzan con el sol.»

En ese momento
La Rosa se sonrío
Al ver unas chistas tracaleras
Que volaban de una palma a un mezquite.

Por fin me dijo:
«Y yo floreo
Con tus palabras
Y poesía.»

En Buscas

I began
In search of words
To relieve myself by expressing
The feelings of my
Fathers and mothers of years past.

A book.
Actually, books and books
Of verse —
Poetry on the Rose of Blood and of pure water
I was to write.

I looked at the sky
And I saw the sun clothe himself
With passing clouds.

Amid the tears of light
Which fell at noon
I saw
The Rose of Blood
Drink its cup of pure water.

Upon seeing me, the flower
Told me:
"Your father and mother
live in the earth,
Run in the water,
Climb on the clouds,
And cast their light with the sun

In that moment
The Rose smiled
At seeing some chattering sparrows
Who flew from a palm tree to a mesquite.
Finally, the rose told me:
"And I bloom
With your words,
And poetry."

Al Amar

yo estaba bañado en obscuridad
en nada
cuando vi una luz tan brillante que
cerré mis ojos
pero la luz penetro
mis párpados.

y sentí el dolor
el dolor de amar y ser
amado.

Al Amar (Upon Loving)

I was bathed in darkness
in nothingness
when I saw a light so bright
I closed my eyes.
The light penetrated through
my eyelids.

And I felt the pain
the pain of loving and of
being loved.

Grace

To see with grace
Is seeing
After God removes
An onion skin
From our eyes.

Then we can truly see
What has always been
There to see —
God's fingerprints
In all things.

Rain

Blue-gray clouds,
barely clinging to the horizon,
hover across the zigzagging
hills and mountains,
riding the cool,
frigid breaths of a blue wind.
Silent and clacking raindrops
tumble
pounce on my windowpane.
Rain, rain, crystal-droplets
splatter on the ledge,
running,
racing,
quenching.

Darkness, sunlight-glare,
are your fingers struggling
for the transparent coat of falling rain?
Must there be darkness, pain, in our
struggles?
Loss and sorrow, laughter and smiles,
where do you embrace?

Heaven, heaven, why aren't you
here on earth,
rather than up there somewhere?

Clickity, clackity,
Falling rain
Sizzles on my window ledge,
Keeping time.
Split, splat, split, splat,
crystal-droplets shattering, splashing
then embracing in swirling pools.
Running,
racing,
quenching.

Mi Ángel

An angel lazily floated in the sky.
his grey veil
moist with rain drops
gently fell on the thirsty grass below.

He scratched his head
and playfully tossed his silver gray hair
that captivated the sun's smile.
while teasing the trees
with his cool breath
he knelt on the hill to pray to the heavens.

Spreading his wings
he kissed the earth
and gracefully flew towards the west
where he met the others
and quietly left.

Order Form

Please send me _____ copies of <u>Wrestling with the Angel — a Collection of Poetry</u> at $11.95 each to

Name_____

Address_____

City _____ State _____

Zip Code _____

_____ copies at $11.95 each = $_____

Sales Tax. 8.25 % CA residents $_____

Shipping Charge $_____

Total Enclosed $_____

Shipping: Book rate, $2 for the first book and 75 cents for each additional book. Please allow three to four weeks for surface mail. Air mail, $3.50 per book.

Please send order form and make check or money order payable to:

Pluma Productions
1977 Carmen Ave.
Los Angeles, CA 90068